Anybody See My Shoes?

Anybody See My Shoes?

Poetic
Reflections From A Chaplain

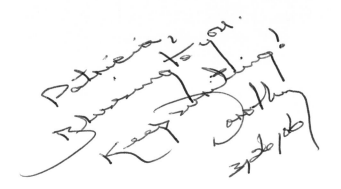

Dorothy Shelly

Foreword by Donna Schaper
Author of *Sabbath Sense* and *Sacred Speech*
Cover artwork by Susan Hashagen.

Library of Congress Number: 2005903665
ISBN: Hardcover   1-59926-248-7
               Softcover   1-4134-9382-3

This book was printed in the United States of America.

To order additional copies of this book, contact:
Xlibris Corporation
1-888-795-4274
www.Xlibris.com
Orders@Xlibris.com
26216

Contents

Acknowledgments 13

Foreword 15

Introduction 17

The Benediction 19

Hold Me 20

Like You Did 21

Invitation To Grace 23

The Saddest Whisper 24

The Carpenter 25

She Knew 26

Reservation 27

What Is It? 29

Nana, Will Jesus . . . . ? 30

Ninety-Six and 31

It's All Right 32

Joy In the Presence of Angels 33

Sacred Silence 35

Jesus Must Have Liked That 36

Unexpected Blessing 38

Open To All 39

What Brought the Tears? 41

Why God, Why? 42

A Ministry of Presence 43

Thanks, Tony 44

Faithful Visitor 45

Heartrending Plea 46

I'm Thirsty 47

The Pot Roast 49

Bedside 50

A Gentle Death 51

What's My Purpose? 52

Her Mantra 53
Do It 54
Hostage 55
I know 56
Her Dance 57
Thanks for the Dance 59
Breathe In . . . Hold It 61
Late October Birches 62
Aimless Wander 63
Do You Know Me? 64
Bids For Memories 65
Walks Together 67
Roll Call 68
One More Battle 69
Viola 70
Days Are Getting Shorter 72
Senseless Wait 73
After All These Years 74
Grace and Remembrances 75
Good Warm Tears 76
On the Way 78
Mary Remembered 80
Hear My Lament 83
I Find My Self 85
Morning Prayers 86
Dear God, ... 87
Divine Spectacle 88
Resurrected Silent Stirrings 90
About the Author 93

Dedicated to all care-givers.

May God continue to help you carry your cross
day by day
and
hour by hour.

*And as they were going out, they met a man
from Cyrene, named Simon, and they forced
him to carry the cross.*

Matthew 27:32

In memory of

Mom

1923-1980

Thank you for all you were to me.
Thank you for what your memories
continue to be for me.

You're already Home
making it nice for when
I come.
Carly Simon
"Like A River"

Earth's crammed with heaven,
And every common bush afire with God,
And only he who sees takes off his shoes;
The rest sit around and pluck blackberries.

Elizabeth Barrett Browning
(1806-1861)

Acknowledgments

Most of these writings were put to paper while ministering with the elderly at a long-term care facility in Upper Bucks County, in eastern Pennsylvania. I am grateful for this setting of ministry that continues to spiritually nourish me. Several people have motivated me to expose the poet within my heart and soul. I especially recall the Reverend Wanda Craner, my spiritual director. Her nurturing has fueled my creative output. In undeniable and unforgettable ways, she helps me to reach deep within my soul. I mention, also, the Reverend Allan Kramer-Moyer, my colleague in pastoral ministry, as well as Donna Elyse, my beloved daughter and best friend. Their encouragement and support have been and continue to be a true blessing. I am also indebted to the Reverend Stephanie Anne Thompson for her wise counsel and unfailing friendship. Others, too, know my gratitude for always believing in me. Elyse Fox has inspired and enriched my life early on in my nursing journey. Likewise, Rebecca Kesselring has inspired and enriched my life early on in my chaplaincy journey. I cannot begin to thank them enough. This page would not be complete without expressing thanks to Elinore Gold who shares her love and enthusiasm for *Poetry With the Pastor*. My heartfelt appreciation also goes out to the residents, for it is they who have given the poems their inspirational essence. Finally, I give thanks for the Spirit within that persistently nudges me to explore the beauty and the solace of writing.

Foreword

Dorothy Shelly, when not looking for shoes, is teaching us how to be a chaplain. Her ministry of grace with the elderly and their families shows in the poems (or are they prayers) which follow. The confusion is intentional: we pray and write poems because the very words we hear are often deeply poetic and prayerful. She beckons us to remove our shoes, to read between the lines and explore with her the heart-rending pleas: "Will you hold me?" and "What's My Purpose?" Dorothy skillfully weaves both medicine and theology as she offers us this gift of grace-filled writings.

Bedside often feels like an isolated place, but it is really a front row seat on life and death. Those who are immobile can often tell us all we need to know about mobility. Those who are sick, whether of body, mind, or spirit, can often tell us all we need to know about wellness. We are the recipients of great gifts as we are filled with awe after awe. Rare is the chaplain who leaves the bedside and doesn't thank God for their own next breath. Chaplains are pushed back towards life ferociously. We are not people who fail to appreciate every little blessing we have been given.

Chaplains are privileged to walk on hallowed ground. It is a job most people don't envy. But, there is something very holy that embraces the chaplain's role. It is a ministry of presence during loss, transition, and change. It is all about meeting people wherever they are on their spiritual journey and getting a sense of where their next step may take them.

I spend a lot of time in nursing homes. I am a pastor. Just recently I tried to smile at a half dozen wheelchair-bound residents in the hall at Amherst Extended Care Center and I failed. No one seemed interested in my self-protecting smile. I stopped smiling, made my visit, endured my parishioner's assuring me that she couldn't hear a word I said but was glad I came and hoped I would go now because she was going to lunch. It was early evening. I bid her an abrupt farewell. She did not realize it was abrupt. Such confusion is important for the conscious to see: it may be our own destination. As is usual in such visits, I gain much from my parishioner.

Chaplains do have an important and vital role today. Long term care facilities, especially faith-based, must be spiritually literate while not spiritually controlling. Serving all faiths and denominations, chaplains must be attuned to hearing and speaking all languages. Make no mistake: chaplains are integral players on the health-care team. They make space in the facility for all that may be unintentionally overlooked, all that can't be priced or evaluated.

Chaplains continue to find warmth in cold spaces as they address questions of meaning, morality and mortality. "Life," as one of my 90-year-old friends just wrote, "is a long feast that awaits the next long feast." What do we do in those times when we don't know what to do or what to say? Like the writer, we look for missing shoes. And we pray. And we let the poet in us overtake us. We know that prose is not enough for the great praying and poetry in life. Dorothy shares, with the reader, her gifts . . . her numerous invitations to grace, her joys in the presence of angels, and her unexpected blessings.

The Reverend Donna Schaper is the pastor of North Hadley Congregational (UCC) Church in Massachusetts. Among her most recent books is "Sacred Speech: A Guide for Keeping Spirit In Your Speech" from SkyLight Press, Woodstock, VT.

Introduction

I enjoy talking with very old people. They have gone before us on a road by which we too may have to travel, and I think we do well to learn from them what it is like, easy or difficult, rough or smooth . . .

Socrates in Plato's Republic

"Take off your shoes; the place where you are standing is holy ground," said the voice of God to Moses. In my ministry with the elderly, I convey that God still speaks those words today. It is my hope that they, regardless of their present life situation, recognize every moment as sacred. It is holy ground; like the place where Moses stood before the burning bush and was privileged to hear God's words.

In essence, as a chaplain I invite my residents to remove their shoes and share their stories. Feelings are evoked and precious memories are stirred. More often than not, after hearing their recollections, I am the recipient of new perspectives on life and its divine meaning. Their sacred sharings have successfully exposed my authentic self. I have once again come face to face with knowing fulfillment in my calling to a ministry with the aged.

Memories of my own journey come flooding back as I hear stories told and retold of tender love as well as tenuous moments. I believe that we all are earthen vessels; repositories of these memories of life experiences until we, too, finally stand upon that sacred place and hear the holy invitation, "Take off your shoes."

As my collection of poems grew, the dream of doing a book began to make headway and unfold. I have brought to this book some of my personal history as well as my professional training as both a registered nurse and a chaplain. These sacred re-creations have brought feelings out of my heart and on to paper. Author Donna Schaper's wisdom, advice, and encouragement spurred me on from her first workshop I attended. Undoubtedly, she has been a motivational force that inspired me to affirm my muse.

In compiling this book, I have been living out my innermost passion. Seeing and holding the finished product is pure happiness for me. Now I rejoice, as did Dorothy Sayers, English scholar and writer, upon finishing a novel, an essay, or a poem who said, "I feel like God on the Seventh Day." Indeed I do.

My hope is that these humble writings stimulate your interest and curiosity. My hope is that, with the eye of your imagination and the ear of your heart, you see and hear the persons within each story. My sincere hope is that these writings will nudge your memories to come alive as you, too, accept the invitation, "Take off your shoes."

The Benediction

"Anybody see my shoes?"
    That's what she called aloud
            At close of *Morning Prayers.*

Coming from way in the back,
    The words seemed to echo . . . .
            "A n y b o d y s e e m y s h o e s?"

Others who gathered complained,
    Claiming it to be a most inappropriate outburst.
To the contrary thought the chaplain.
    It was a holy benediction.

Florence comes to *Morning Prayers,*
    Sees the glow and feels the warmth
            Of the burning bush.

Clearly it is she, not the chaplain,
    Who pronounces the benediction . . . .
            "Anybody see my shoes?"

> *Take the sandals from your feet,*
> *for the place on which you are*
> *standing is holy ground.*
> Exodus 3:5

Hold Me

I sat there on the old bench . . . .
  Sorting my thoughts,
        Pondering the meaning of a ministry
        On the dementia unit.

Beside me sat Anne
  Gibber-jabbering as usual,
        God only knows what.
A mind seemingly in perpetual motion
  And devastated by scattered emotions.
      Suddenly, with eyes catching mine
         And like a child in distress, she whispered,
           "Will you hold me?"

That moment,
  that very moment,
        This humbled chaplain was led into sacred space . . . .
        Into that quiet place beside still waters.

> . . . *he leads me beside still waters;*
> *he restores my soul.*
>
> *Psalm 23:2b*

Like You Did

Bid me to come,
  Put me on your knee and bless me,
      like you did the little children.

Teach me to pray,
  Still my anxious thoughts,
      like you did the twelve.

Give me a drink,
  Quench my spiritual thirst,
          like you did the Samaritan woman.

Reach for my hand,
  Pull me to safety,
          like you did Peter.

Open my eyes,
  Give light to my darkness,
          like you did Bartimaeus.

Weep for me,
  Show me your grace,
          like you did Lazarus.

Call me by name,
  Surprise me in the garden,
          like you did Mary.

Walk with me,
  Urge me to touch your wounds,
        like you did Thomas.

Wait for me on the shore,
  Invite me to come and have breakfast,
        like you did the fishermen.

Invitation To Grace

With pure white hair swept into an elegant twist,
  Unmatched by a face of deep wrinkles from growing age,

Strangely quiet, Winifred stood peering at the nurse behind the desk,
  As if begging for grace.

No spoken words . . . only heavy sighs and grimaces
  Conveying some secret silent aches.

Breaking the ominous silence . . .
  Attempting to explain my role as chaplain,
        While realizing her limited understanding, I whispered,
          "Winnie, I have been sent here to pray for you."

Tears of relief brought soft-spoken words,
  "No one ever said that to me before."

The Saddest Whisper

I want to go home.

Alone,
  Forgotten,
    Displaced,
      Abandoned,
       Uprooted,
        Discarded,
                and Cast-out.

The body is present.
        The heart is absent.

Searching for *home* within a wilderness.

The most painful ache of the aged,

  Heard again,

                  again,
            and still again.

    I want to go home.

    The saddest whisper.

*They were longing for a better country—
a heavenly one. Therefore God is not
ashamed to be called their God, for He
has prepared a city for them.*

Hebrews 11:16

The Carpenter

My father was a carpenter,
  She said spontaneously.
          Words came from out of nowhere.

So was my father.
  The chaplain responded,
          Merely to spur conversation.

And so was Jesus, she exhorted,
  And so was Mary's Joseph.

          Words came no more from either.
                  Just hallowed silence, matching smiles,
          And a twinkle in her eye.

She Knew

It would be wool
  And it would be pink.

She wanted a scarf.
  She needed a scarf.
        She knew.

Pure virgin wool,
  Wool to keep her warm.
Bright pink,
  Pink her favorite color.

It was Monday.
  Who thought Friday would take her?
        She did.
            It did.

                  She knew.

Reservation

A face radiating with grace
  And a frail aged body.
A mind of keen insight
  That conveyed candid wisdom
          As she pondered her mortality.

Well into her ninth decade of life,
  When coming to the nursing home.
          She did so without complaint or regret.

This time of change and transition,
  This time of introspection,
          She grieved not for loss of home
          And material possessions.

Rather, she lamented the distance
  Between her and her only daughter.
          Aching with every word,
            Spoken and unspoken.
          Yearning for her nearness,
            At this time of soul-searching.

Just not herself this morning,
  Informing staff of her reservation to leave
          Later this day . . . this Friday evening.

Her determination was convincing,
   Persisting until a hair appointment was moved up.
      (Just like any woman with plans.)
Reassuring all of her anticipated departure.
   The reservation was a sure thing,
         In her mind's eye.
Ready to soon take leave
   And no one could tell her differently.

This evening, this very evening death came.
   Death came gently for her,
            This ninety-something woman
               Of straight-forward wisdom and resilient spirit,

               Who was most certain . . . .
                           Certain of her reservation.

What Is It?

What is it, God?
  What is it?

Show me.
  Take me.
    Lead me.
      Open my eyes.

Tell me.
  Whisper it.
    Shout it.
      Attune my ears.

Impart your omniscient wisdom.
  Show me.
    Tell me.
      Enlighten me.

Equip me for this ministry.
  Let me see.
    Let me hear,
      This still more excellent way.

What is it, God?
  What is it?

But eagerly desire the greater gifts. And now
I will show you the most excellent way.
I Corinthians 12:31

Nana, Will Jesus . . . . ?

Solemn, sacred minutes
  Seeming like hours.
Watching, waiting, and wondering . . . .
  Would the next shallow breath
          Be the one, the last?

Bedside vigil with John.
  Wife, daughter and husband,
          Present with the chaplain.

Profound stillness.
  Silence broken only by
          An occasional audible breath.

Stillness,
      quietness,
          and silence.

Still, quiet, and silent.
  Still, quiet, and silent until,
          Until three year old Kerstin arrived.
          And we all heard it . . . .
          spontaneous words of wisdom,
            as her little hands blotted Nana's tears,

Will Jesus . . . .
      soon be sending one of his cars for Great Grand-Pop?

                    . . . and a little child shall lead them.
                    Isaiah 11:6

Ninety-Six and . . . .

Looking up at the nurse
  Grimacing with pain . . . .
            Radiating and unrelenting,
                Unrelieved by Nitroglycerin.

Life-color slowly fading . . . .
  Obvious to staff at bedside
            Looking down on her,
                Eagerly ready to do something.

She holds tight the chaplain's hand,
  In search of meaning and solace.

The young EMT demands;
  "Sarah, Sarah, can you hear me?
            How old are you?"

            In a strained whisper came:
"I'm ninety-six and wouldn't wish it on anyone!"

It's All Right

Anne is her name,
Though in her delusions she's *Mary*
Along with her daughter,
And all those who care for her.

Staff say *Mary* was her mother's name.
So calls for *MARY, MARY* go out to everyone,
Loud and distinct cries,
Demands of deep angst.

Whispered words from the chaplain . . . .
"Have no fear . . . . It's all right, *Mary*."

Message of sacred assurance
Heard long ago by another Mary
In the foretelling of a miraculous birth.
Message of sacred assurance
Heard long ago by another Mary
At an empty tomb in a garden.

"Have no fear . . . .
It's all right, Mary.

It's all right."

Joy In the Presence of Angels

One hundred sheep
  Ten coins
    Two sons

Sheep
  Coin
    Son

Lost
  Found
    Rejoice

      Third Gospel text exegesis
       with a personal glimpse back.

Losses . . . .

    Bracelet . . . special gift
      Ring . . . belonged to an older sister
        Pet dog . . . Lassie-like Collie
          Friend . . . bonded since childhood
            Parents . . . too soon
              Child . . . NO words could console
                Good health . . . dimness of vision, hardness of hearing
              Strength . . . weakening body
                Independence . . . with much resistence

Loss most feared . . .
         "My mind"
Spontaneous words coming from Mabel,
    The ninety-year-old amputee in the front row
       of the weekly Bible study group.

Once again this chaplain has felt it,
    "Joy in the presence of angels of God."

Sacred Silence

As a young spirited girl,
  She spoke those words often,
    "Wish I could go!"
Words said in haste as a plea
  To do, to search, to explore, to live,
    To experience life—all of it.

Now as a weary, yet grace-filled woman
  Whose aged features truthfully impart
    Her ninth decade of life.

No longer facing days with youthful vigor,
  Though still with yearning spirit
    And straight-forward wisdom,
She says with a deep sigh,
  "Wish I could Go!"

No murmured words of encouragement
  From the listening chaplain,
    Instead, with discerning eyes,

    We sifted through the *sacred silence.*

Jesus Must Have Liked That

An outward and visible sign of the grace of God,
  Water and the Holy Spirit.
    Buried *with* and raised *from* . . .
      To life's newness.

A sign and seal
  Of God's forgiveness and acceptance,
A celebration
  Of Christ's presence,
A promise
  To follow,
    To resist,
          To show,
            To witness,
            To grow.

Strength, courage, joy, freedom, and hope,
  Through a blessing given to all.

She was impulsive to wander and stray,
  With delusional adventures
    And cruel mental incapacities,
      Triggered by disrupted neuronal patterns
        Secondary to cerebral plaques and tangles.

Somehow, somehow,
  Water touched to the forehead
    Prompted her to stay . . . .
      Memories of earlier years flooded back.

Gracie, more often mute and downcast,
  Inhibited by steady, involuntary Parkinson tremors,
    Looks up at the chaplain with smile and words:
      "Jesus must have liked that."

Unexpected Blessing

Arthritis has crippled her hands.
Rigid fingers bent at nearly right angles,
　Effects of inflamed joints,
　　Joints no longer purposeful.

Stroke has rendered her speechless.
Meaningful words no longer spoken,
　Though not unable to communicate,
　　Through a spontaneous never-ending smile.

Reaching to shake her hand,
　After whispered words;
　　"Peace of Christ be with you."
Suddenly feeling her pull,
　My face to hers,
　　Graced upon my left cheek
　　　Was a big wet kiss.

Truly,
　From Clara,
　　An unexpected blessing.

Open To All

Wheat and grapes,
  Bread and wine,
Paten and chalice,
  Vessels of life and labor.

A loaf, a fresh loaf still warm, baked by Jan,
  Friend and nurse who brings to life her special recipe
    Only for the Eucharist.
A cup, a special cup, hand thrown and glazed by Tom,
  Friend and colleague in ministry who personalized it
    With my initials and Ordination date.

Invitation and call
  To the supper,
Celebration of a past meal
  And the future heavenly banquet.

      One in body
        And one in the church.

Visible breaking of the bread
  And audible pouring of the wine.
    Holding the sacred elements high,
      So all gathered could see God's gifts.

The blessing.
  All things are now ready.

And then, then it happened . . . .
Suddenly the somber smiles turned to laughter.
Chattering prevailed as fingers pointed to the makeshift altar . . . .
An over-bed table draped with a white starched draw sheet.

Buckwheat, the beloved black cat residing with the Alzheimer folks,
Has now found peace and solace
Lying upon the Communion table.

Sighs of relief from the congregation,
As his outstretched body gracefully embraced the symbols,
While the chaplain reminded her congregants;
"This table is open to ALL."

What Brought the Tears?

Blessed bread and wine,
  Broken and poured,
    Distributed and partaken by all.

Prayer of thanksgiving,
  Giving thanks for the invitation,
    The presence of Christ,
      And all his gifts.

Clearing the draped table,
  I heard the sobs
    And saw the tears of Alice.

Tears later dried with my white stole
  and consolation received from a question . . . .
    "Alice, what brought the tears?"

> *"I don't know; but thank you.*
> *Thank you for bringing them."*

> *He will wipe away every tear from their eyes.*
> *There will be no more death or mourning or*
> *crying or pain, for the old order of things*
> *has passed away.*
> Revelation 21:4

Why God, Why?

I was half way there,
  Almost finally Home.
Why was I stopped?
  Why did God bring me back here?

I was half dead,
  Almost finally there.
Why couldn't I leave?
  Why didn't God let me go?

I should be there.
  I should be There.
Why am I still here?
  Why God?
                        WHY?

A Ministry of Presence

I sat with him in silence . . . .
        and watched and pondered.

    Drips of nourishment
       through a needle in a withered hand
          scarcely sustained his frail body.
    Weary eyes, labored breathing
       and a wrinkled brow
          conveyed overt signs of strife.
    Failed attempts at turning racing, twisted thoughts
       into meaningful words and . . .
          color indicative of losing life's battle.

       The victor will soon prevail

I sat with him in silence . . . .
        and watched and pondered.

Thanks, Tony

Wednesday again . . . It's Wednesday again,
  Program day in the Alzheimer's Unit.
Would I keep their attention today?
  Would I even capture their attention?
My olive wood statues of those three gift-bearing Wise Men
  Just might help . . . resurrect and rediscover
    The old, old Epiphany story.

Sitting in silence until the scent of frankincense and myrrh
  Oil of anointing touched to the forehead.
Transported back by memories of childhood,
  Tony, in his mind, was at Christmas Eve midnight mass.

    Just a small parish, near the Duna River,
      A little village in Hungary.
    Hand in hand with mother,
      Standing in the bitter cold,
        Hoping to get a seat when inside.
        (Everyone went this night to pay homage.)

His sharing came not without tears.
  Those memories of former days
    When he too would later depart another way . . .
      Searching diligently for God in that Russia camp . . . four long years.

Another Wednesday . . .
  Another glimpse of an epiphany.

              Thanks, Tony.
              Thanks.

Faithful Visitor

They shared life together
  Fifty plus seven vibrant years.

Downcast, alone and with feelings of guilt,
  He faithfully visits her daily.

Will she recognize him this day
  Or think him to be a stranger in her midst?
Will she perceive him as father, brother, son
  Or, again, as the unwanted intruder?

He talks day after day
  About everything that happened up to now.

Like the two on their seven mile journey
  To that village called Emmaus,
May she, too, know him
  As a companion on the way.

Will the story be unfolded for her,
  As for them through the breaking of bread
    When love was recognized?

God, warm her heart,
  Open her eyes again
    Just once again for him,
      Her faithful visitor.

*Then their eyes were opened
and they recognized him; . . . .*
Luke 24:31

Heartrending Plea

A small hunched-over,
　Frail, aged figure.

A mind oblivious to the no-cure
　Disease of devastation . . .
　　　　　　　　Alzheimer's.

Quick, short breaths
　Through dry, pursed lips
　　Until the determined words spew forth . . .
　　"Will you?
　　　Will you be my friend?
　　　Will you be my friend today?"

Stopping to rest her head
　On my shoulder,
　Only to repeat it again,
　　Her heartrending plea . . .

　　Will you be my friend?

　　　　　　　Fear not, for I am with you,
　　　　　　　be not dismayed, for I am
　　　　　　　your God; . . . .
　　　　　　　　　Isaiah 41:10

I'm Thirsty

Outstretched hands
  With opened palms
To receive the blessed
  Bread and wine.
      Ready and waiting.

Edna came, this time, to the table.

No wandering
  Or disturbed behavior
No disruptive chatter
  Or, seemingly, memory loss.

Rather,
  Stillness, connectedness
    Emotional awareness,
      With sensory appreciation.

Liturgical remembrance
  Of words and the Word,
Memories that re-present
  That memorial sacrament.

Telling of that Last Supper story,
  Eucharistic liturgy,
    Paten of broken whole wheat bread,
      Chalice of sweet concord grape Manischewitz,
        Single lit candle illuminating a tarnished cross,
          And the *Our Father* heard from Anne Murray's *Inspirational Classics.*
God's Christ was, indeed, present.

Not a word was spoken,
  Until she sipped from the little cup,
    I'm thirsty.
      Give me more! I'm thirsty!
                        Come, all you who are thirsty, ...
                              Isaiah 55:1

The Pot Roast

A dream shared
  Before his last night.

      Seeing his wife in Paradise
          And the Sunday dinner table set.
      All is ready,
          All is now ready,
              Except for the pot roast.

      She repeats . . . .
          It's not done.
              It's not done.
                  It's not done, yet.
                      The pot roast is not done.

"Come to the table," Christ said.

      Go, Bill, accept the gracious invitation.

      The pot roast is now done.

Bedside

Another long vigil ended
No longer living on the threshold.
No longer the frail grasp on this life.

Again, again we're here
This holy place and sacred time,
bedside with the deceased.

Gathered with stinging tears,
Chaplain, family and staff,
Her half of a not-so-spacious room.
The side without the window.

Jesus is here again, too.
Hearing what is not spoken
And seeing what is not visible.

He has honored us with his presence,
In the faces of all around the bedside.

A Gentle Death

No frightening hi-tech medical gadgetry.
  No beeping life-support machinery.
    No complex curative measures.
      No waiting professionals eager to 'jump-start'
      the failing heart.
      No mental battle over pulling plugs.
      No isolation.

Rather . . .
  An aura of bonding between family members
    keeping bedside vigil.
      Sharing memories—remembering when . . . . ,
      Sharing feelings—letting go with grace.
    The presence of a chaplain
      whispering words of assurance and comfort.

A final breath
  A sudden pain of reality
    A stillness
      A quietness
        A peacefulness
            Tears

It was gentle . . . .
        A gentle death.

What's My Purpose?

Vintage damask linen
  On a mahogany dining room table,
    Set with Grand Buffet flatware,
      and a centerpiece of fragrant yellow roses,
        hybrid cuttings from the back garden.
Lit white taper candles
  Adorning the aged curly oak sideboard,
Warm whole wheat bread
  Baked in old ironstone,
Savory home-cooking
  Served on mother's Wedgewood,
Steaming Irish coffee
  With cream on top,
    In hand-painted China cups,
Angel food cake
  Made from scratch,
      and, of course, Scotch whiskey
          Offered in good crystal,
              Only the very best for Father Fitzgerald.

Now . . . .
  No table or even a paper napkin for you!

Tell me.
  Tell me chaplain,
        What is it?

        What's my purpose?

Her Mantra

Spoken aloud from dawn 'till dusk,
  Distillations of spiritual wisdom.

Beyond all doubt, profound words of lament,
  Unsolicited insight from a centenarian-plus-four.

    When I'm home,
      It'll be better.
        When I'm Home,
          It'll be better . . . .

                              It'll be better.

                    "I will go before you and will
                    level the mountains."
                              Isaiah 45:2

Do It

Do to others
  Like you would
    Have them do to you.

Just do it!
  If you can't,
    Step aside.

        And you will have no *troubleation*.

But, do it.
  Just do it.
    Do it.

      Do it!

Hostage

How?
  How can you?
    How can you say this is a religious place?
                              Ruth demanded.

All the doors are locked.
  I'm a hostage!
              I'm a hostage!

Others, too, long ago knew that fear
  Of being behind locked doors.

  Only soon to realize . . .
                No barred doors
                    Could keep out the Risen Christ.
                No closed doors
                    Could stop his presence.
                No shut doors
                    Could stop his blessing—
                "Peace be to you."

Peace.
        Peace be to you,
                              Ruth.

I know . . . .

The artist just finished her masterpiece
  A pristine mural of mellow late summer sky,
    Tasseled corn, white picket fence—
      The backrest for pastel lupines
        And a stop-over for a contemplative ladybug,
      Rustic birdhouse with nesting finch,
        And, in the distance, a farmer's red barn.

A beautiful work of art
  On the doors.
A visual resting place
  Created with hopes of deterring
    Exit-seeking behavior
      On the Alzheimer Unit.

Who would know?
  Who would ever guess?

Ruth, what do you think?
        (Hands on hips while pondering
            the young artist's question . . .)

          I know.
            I know!
              I know those damn doors are locked!

              I'm still a hostage!

Her Dance

Family says, "Don't tell . . . .
  Don't tell mother she's dying."
              Can't tell her she's inching closer,
              Closer, and closer to death.

What do I say
  If she asks, "Am I dying?"
              What will I say?
              What *will* I say?

She knows.
  She's ready.

  Let's dance.
              Let's dance, Catherine.
  It's your dance.
              You lead and I'll follow.

  Dance.
              Dance, Catherine.
        Lead me right up to Heaven's gates
      And I'll twirl you into his waiting arms . . . .
              The soldier husband waiting since '45.

She knows.
  She's ready.

    We're dancing,
        one
          step
            at a
              time.

              We're d a n c i n g,
                    d a n c i n g...

Thanks for the Dance

A still peaceful Monday morning
  Early March and seeming spring-like
      in spite of the layer of fresh snow under foot.

An old rural cemetery
  Just outside the village
      in pristine Upper Bucks County,
          Stone markers as far back as a century or two.

The five of us solemnly gathered,
  Including the quiet, unassuming undertaker
      and excluding the one with shovel in hand,
          In the too near distance, waiting to finish.

A pair of inquisitive Mourning Doves
  Offering up an occasional moan,
Several lively Chickadees
  Beckoning with welcoming hospitality.
Bright sun warming our faces
  And its light turning tears to glistening diamonds.

Scriptures, prayers of thanksgiving
  Followed by silence, the Prayer of Our Savior,
      the commendation of her ashes, then Simeon's words,
          Readings of poetry, blessings, and a benediction.

With aromatic burning sage, cradled by a tortoise shell,
  And calling Canada Geese in flight,
        her son gently lifted the blue marble treasure chest
            And carefully placed it in the small earthen hole.
Meticulously he shoveled the fresh mound of dirt
  Around and on top, consummating the ritual
        with flat spruce twigs as her blanket.

We exchanged hugs and parted.
  Turning away, I whispered, "Thanks,
                    Thanks for the dance, Catherine."

Breathe In . . . Hold It

Shock, denial, shock,
  Disbelief . . . No. Can't be.
Nervous, anxious, afraid,
  Wakeful nights, fretful days . . . Waiting.

Poking, pushing, pressing,
  Squashing, squeezing,
X-rays, ultrasound, x-rays,
  Biopsy, x-rays again . . . Waiting.

Questions, concerns, conjectures,
  Suspicions, unknowns.
Worry—one in eight . . . ,
          Trust, pray . . . Wait.

    Finally . . .
      Peace,
        Blessed reality,

        Benign . . . fibroid.

      Breath out.

Late October Birches

Like the late October birches
  Whose golden pinnate leaves have fallen,
      Her mood has also dropped.

Like those naked trees,
  She, too, is empty and hollow.

With growing darkness of shortened days,
  Her spirit retreats in silent pensive reflection.

With change of seasons,
  She, too, shifts . . .
      Self-loathing and complacency have surfaced.

As cold winter's intrusion nears,
  Her world turns bleakly melancholic.

    God, hold her up and stand her tall,
      As she once again patiently awaits
        To be graced by the light and warmth
          of spring,

    Like the late October birches.

In the shadow of your wings, I will take refuge,
until the destroying storms pass by.
               Psalm 57:1

Aimless Wander

No. No!
  Get out!
       Get out of here!
         It's not your room!

Meandering,
  Shuffled pace,
    Uncertain of a next step or turn,
      Lingering where he shouldn't

Vacant stare,
  Distant affect,
    Inappropriate smile,
      Poor boundaries,
        Lost identity

Like an endless wilderness search.

      Everyday trials of dementia devastation.

God knows
  And God remembers.

      God knows Russ
        and the way to his room.

Even to your old age and gray hair I am He,
I am He who will sustain you. I have made
you and I will carry you; I will sustain you
and I will rescue you.

Isaiah 46:4

Do You Know Me?

She visits faithfully
  Day after day, same time,
      as sure as the sun's rising and setting.

Love of her life. None other.
  He's the only one,
      together since '45.

She sees him the same,
  Warm feelings remain,
      time after time, with each glance.

But, this day
  She's not sure.
      The question must be asked.

Do you know me?
  Do you know my name?

With eyes catching her's
  And a voice of clarity,
      As if the dementia had momentarily fled,

     I don't know your name;
      but, I do know that I love you!

Bids For Memories

They came for the auction,
  Family, friends and strangers.
All curious . . .
  What did she have?
    What would it go for?

Cherished memories
  Spread upon blue tarps
    Covering nearly three acres.
Quilts, draped over porch railing and wash line,
  Intricately sewn years back
    When she still had her sight.

Blue Willow dishes and a complete set of Fiesta Ware,
  A round hall mirror, superb cut glass, and ordinary paintings,
    Sought now for their old frames,
      And many more wedding gifts
        Received back in '33.

A vintage player piano,
  That graced the parlor with melody,
    And cases of Imperial music rolls,
      That will soon go on e-Bay
        To a much higher bidder.

Boxes of books
  Some with hand-written messages,
    Words of love and encouragement.
All sorts of books
  From *The Good Book*
    To *The Complete Book of Composting*
      And seemingly all in between.

The old two-seater porch swing,
  With matching green metal chairs,
    (Now called 'motel' chairs,)
      All fetched a good price.
Tools used by the carpenter, farmer, and gardener.
  Most knew the grip of her hands, too,
    Before crippling arthritis set in.
All fetched a good price.
  Who would have thought?
    Who would have ever thought?

Toys, the simple wind-up kind,
  Board games, marbles, and jacks,
    No electronic gadgets or soft-ware
      To be found here.

A white porcelain kitchen table,
  With black edging and chrome legs,
    Still shines like new,
      Once the meeting spot for family sharing.

"Did you know her?
  Do you know her?
    Did she die?
      Is she in a nursing home?"

The chaplain's response was interrupted
  With the sudden raising of the man's card, #33,
    Highest bidder for the old, round hall mirror.

I do know her . . .
  Have known Elsie since my childhood.

      Yes, she's content . . . .
                    at peace in the home.

Walks Together

Fifty-some years ago,
  She tied his shoes, closed his jacket
    And took him by the hand.
      Together they walked.
        With each small step came his protest,
          "Mommy, I don't want to go.
            I don't want to go to school!"

Fifty-some years later,
  He ties her shoes, closes her jacket
    And takes her by the arm.
      Together they guide the walker.
        With each shuffled step comes her lament,
          "Son, I don't want to go.
        I don't want to go to day-care!
        I'll pay you for NOT taking me!"

*". . . but when you are old you will stretch out
your hands, and someone else will dress you
and lead you where you do not want to go."*
                    John 21:18b.

Roll Call

When the trumpet of the Lord shall sound,
        and time shall be no more,
and the morning breaks, eternal, bright and fair; . . . .

Last time I sang those words with a chaplain,
        I went into battle.
                The year was 1943
                And I'll never forget it.

    I was one of them . . .
        Torpedo-man
            on a Hamul class Destroyer Tender,
                14,900 tons and 492 feet
                    Powerful guns, heavy combat armor
                        Great precision, hit targets more than 30km
                            Seaworthy vessel, "Daughter of the Stars"

Long way from New London
  Long way from Bremerton

Got religion fast
  Out there in the Pacific
                On that floating powder keg.

When the roll is called up yonder.
When the roll is called up yonder.
When the roll is called up yonder.
When the roll is called up yonder,
            I'll be there.
                James M. Black

One More Battle

Most now in life's eighth decade,
　Veterans gathered for their day of honor.

Following words of prayer,
　Red carnations were pinned
　　as the chaplain called roll . . . .

　　　　Edgar S.—Army
　　　　　Donald R.—Navy
　　　　　Norman B.—Army
　　　　　　Eva Marie S.—Army, Women's Air Corps . . . . .

Then it happened.
　I was certain.
　　Her radiant smile, bright eyes,
　　　And flowing tears . . . they told me so.

For one brief moment, just one moment,
　She knew.
　　She understood.
　　　She was present.

Robbed of nearly all reality awareness,
　Still fighting though.
　　One more battle . . . . dementia.

　　　　Eva was still fighting one more,
　　　　　One more battle.

Viola

Small flower with rays of deep color
  Looking like an ever smiling face
    making itself known in May.

Heart-shaped leaves
  Resembling opened hands,
Fine, sweetly scented roots
  Anchoring and supporting.

Lover of full sun
  this *Lady's Flower of Humility*,
Prolific in bloom
  With long flowering seasons.

Small in stature,
  Big on kindness and compassion.
Smiles and laughs,
  Candy and gum.
Gentle of voice,
  Not forceful or direct.
Simple and humble,
  Quiet and unassuming.

Self-giver, always
    Shirt-off-your-back kind.
Springtime in the country,
    Favorite time and place.

Those were the words,
    Words of eulogy for Grand-mom,

            Viola May.

Days Are Getting Shorter

He stares out the window,
  While gripping her hand and saying,
    Days are getting shorter.

Wheezing with each labored breath,
  Keeping pace with the swishing
            Of an oxygen concentrator.

Drops of normal saline,
  Hydrating the frail, aged body.

Dimmed vision,
  Painful left eye,

Bandaged foot, sterile dressings
  covering the non-healing surgical wound.

Will the surgeon be needed again?
  Will the foot be salvaged?

        Ravages of diabetes.

          Was it neglect?
            Or was it denial?

Summer is making way for autumn.
  The season is changing
        And so is he.

Days are getting shorter.
  Days *are* getting shorter, Dad.

Senseless Wait

Why?
   Why after fifty-six years
      Is she still seeking his love?

God of grace, where are You?
   Turn on the light,
      Move her to the dawn,
         Ease the pain,
            Set her free,
               Free to face reality.

She is not orphaned,
   Not some homeless waif;
      But, has your promised Spirit.

Good God, deliver her
   From this wait,
      This senseless tarry,
         This senseless yearning
                        for a father's love.

After All These Years

I love you.
  I love you, too.

Why?
  Why now?

Did he think she understood
  All he didn't say,
    All he never said,
      those unspoken words,
        those unshared feelings?

Why?
  Why now
        After all these years?

I love you.

    I love you, too,
              Dad.

Grace and Remembrances

Like little boys playing with 'tinker toys,'
  They took apart the aged barn.

Beam by beam, once held securely by wooden pegs,
  Cautiously lowered to the frozen ground.

Childhood memories resurrected with each dismantled timber . . .
  Games of make-believe play in the hay-mow
    With friends now grown,
  Sledding down the winter barn hill . . .
Now soon to be leveled.
  Tiger lilies composing a sea of orange,
    Climbing the side of that steep hill.
  Four-leaf clovers . . .
    Discoveries pressed between pages of the family Bible.
  Hollyhocks standing tall against a foundation of stone,
    While fighting the evening breeze,
  Bleeding hearts scattered here and there,
    All succumbed to passing time.

      Lost in nostalgia . . .
        The beauty, the simplicity, the tranquility . . .
          Childhood dreams . . . childhood schemes.

A stately looking weathered barn,
  Age had blessed its walls with character.

      But, like the weeping willow
        felled by lightening years back,
           It, too, has been out-lived by time.

Good Warm Tears

It's mid October,
  One month after my birthday.
    I've seen fifty-seven of them come and go.

Mom, your youngest is now that age,
  That age you were when death came.

My grief then came with passing wonder
  And casual words, "too young and too soon."

With ease I still slip into those memories,
  From, as a little girl, watching you gently care for
    Zinnias, bleeding hearts, and day lilies
  To, as a young woman, hearing your last whispered
    "I love you," to me and my little girl.

Now I know.
  I do know.
    I know for certain.
You were too young
  And it was too soon
                like the early October killing frost
              Taking the zinnias while still in bloom,
          like the late October time change
            Cutting short the light of day.

Too young! Too soon!
    Those words resound within my prayers of lament.

But, like the lilies and the bleeding hearts
   That keep returning,
      So, too, will your memories
         Along with the good warm tears.

For everything there is a season,
and a time for every matter under
Heaven:

Ecclesiastes 3:1

On the Way

Buckwheat, that beloved black cat
  Residing on the Alzheimer's Unit,
More than once has known
  The peace and solace of lying upon
    The chaplain's table of Communion.

With closed eyes and an audible purr,
  His dark and warm out-stretched body
    Half-encircled the chalice and matching paten.

He must have known.
  He, too, must have known
    The sacredness of the holy time.

Called into question, more often than not,
  Is Bucky's therapeutic value,
    As most think of him as
        Being in the way.

Mary Rose in room 304 discovered otherwise
  When she took to her bed and refused to eat
    Nine days before meeting her Maker.

Bucky was no longer in the way;
  But, rather on the way with Mary Rose . . .
    Her security, protection, and soul-nourishment,
      Her antidote to calm and peace.

He abided with her
  As far as he could go,
    Curled up and snuggled against her warm skin,
      Until the funeral director gently lifted him from the bed.

Buckwheat must have known.
  He, too, must have known the sacredness
    Of being on the way with another.

Mary Remembered

Old and *full of days*,
    As the Hebrew scriptures speak of them,
        Are these wise sages who gather
            for the chaplain's poetry hour.

For Mary, one of those favorites
    I know I'm not supposed to have,
        Childhood memories were triggered
            When hearing Thomas Hood's "I Remember."

Quiet, never offered a spoken word until this day
    When others shared growing-up memories
        Of the house, the flowers, the swing, the family . . .
            The place where they grew up.

Longe-quelled memories of former years,
    A voice no longer hushed,
        Eloquent words finally took flight,
                Taking us along on a tender pilgrimage.

She wandered freely back to that place and time
    Thought to be around the early 1920s,
        Bethany, once Manderbach Spring,
            Nestled in woodlands
                Just west of the city of Reading,
                    In Pennsylvania's pristine Berks County

Shaded recollections
   of more than eighty years past
      were now clearly present.
Refreshed and renewed
  like the healthy air
        in that rural village.

A big stone house with a really big kitchen,
  A long oak trestle table where the children gathered.
    And with eyes closed and hands folded,
       All had a turn at leading the mealtime prayer.

Ate a lot of beans and home-made soup.
  Got everything out back in the patch.
    Always had fresh-baked rye bread.
      And no sodas . . .
      Never without spring water,
       Thought to have curative powers,
         coming down the South Mountain.

Picked huckleberries
  'til my fingers were stained black,
    Out beyond the old lilacs on the hillside,
      (Like blueberries only darker and sweeter.)
    Still can smell those pies
      As they cooled on the windowsill.

Refreshing memories of hot summer afternoons
  At the 'old swimming hole' with friends.
    You know, that's where I met him.
    That's where I met my husband.

Sunday School was a must
  And church too, every Sabbath morning,
    Walked together to Bausman Memorial
        And picked wild violets along the way.

Prayers at bedtime were another must
  And then . . .
            Then it was lights out.

Mary never had too much . . . .
        But Mary knew she had much

                                At the children's home.

Hear *My* Lament

Yesterday . . .
  Chaplain, I don't believe in the church;
    But, I do believe in your God.
  When you return tomorrow,
    Will you bring Communion?

Today . . .
  Getting the request together
    Bite-sized squares of bread,
      sweet red wine in little plastic cups.
Preparing to serve and share
  The blessed meal with her,
Listening to messages of voice mail
  I clearly heard it (from the nurse supervisor),
    Doris in 110 died at 0100.
      No family to call.
        Left message for guardian
          At the bank in town.
      Have a good day, chaplain.

Looking intently at the simple meal,
  Staring at those holy elements
        On my desk of clutter,
I knew. I knew for certain.
  She had already received the sacrament
    At a Heavenly banquet
        As God's guest of honor.

Those gates opened wide for her
  And the first face she saw was God
      with arms outstretched for a warm embrace.

But, Lord, now help me.
  Help me in my frailness
      to minister the rest of this day
        As I grapple with the questions.
                Hear *my* lament!

I Find My *Self*

Intimate thoughts that for too long
  Have been tucked away
    Harbored in a safe place
        Known only by me.

Unspoken feelings that when read
  And re-read evoke positive,
    Powerful, yet mystic energy.

Whispered tenderness
  In still, quiet moments.
Honest, genuine talk with me
  That spurs and prods self-affirmation.
    Gone is the self-doubt . . . again.

Heart-felt narratives
  When read aloud,
    The soul becomes undone
      And the Spirit is piqued
      as I find my *self.*

I wonder . . . .
    Dare I cease whispering
    and begin

SHOUTING?

Morning Prayers

Hail Mary! Full of grace,
the Lord is with thee;
blessed are thou among women,
and blessed is the fruit of thy womb, Jesus.
Holy Mary, Mother of God,
pray for us sinners,
now and at the time of our death.

Amen.

Friday, every Friday
  At quarter past ten
    Folks gather.
            Residents of all faiths congregate,
                Coming together for morning prayers.

Friday, every Friday
  This Protestant chaplain prays
        The Hail Mary
  And heard are the whispers:
Hail Mary! Full of grace,
the Lord is with thee;
blessed are thee among women,
and blessed is the fruit of thy womb, Jesus.
Holy Mary, mother of God,
pray for us sinners,
now and at the hour of our death.

Amen.

Friday, every Friday
  We all come together for morning prayers.

Ut unum sint

Dear God,

Bless all who reside here.
　Give them assurance of hope
　　　　with each new morning.
　Strengthen and renew their spirits.
　Still any anxious thoughts about
　　　　tomorrow.
May they find comfort, rest and
　　　　　　peace at the close of each day.

Bless all who labor here.
　Give them wisdom and enthusiasm
　　　　to serve.
　Grant them the grace
　　　　to give
　　　　　and to receive
　　　　to do
　　　　　and to be.

May all within these walls
　feel Your nearness
　　　　and know Your ever-presence.

AMEN.

Divine Spectacle

No poet's pen or artist's brush,
　No photographer's lens or singer's voice
　　　　Could ever justly describe it.

The dark Fall Vermont sky suddenly came alive,
　Over two-lane Route 11 North,
　　　　Before turning left at Priory Hill Road.
　　　　Nearing evening prayers with the Brothers.

What was it?
　Could it?
　　　　Could it be that time?
　　　　Was God about to keep His promise?

The heavens were opening.
　Streams of brilliant lights broke through the darkness.
　　　　Lights of vivid pink, blue, yellow, and green
　　　　With a defining white line between each.

What would Celsius have thought
　Of the luminous phenomenon,
　　　　Of energetic electrons and protons,
　　　　This excited state of the upper atmosphere?

Come morning, it was everyone's breakfast conversation
  At Joe and Pat's Swiss Inn.
Come morning, it was front page for *The Rutland Herald,*
  And a big splash of color.
            On the thirty-first day of October.

Poet, artist, photographer and singer
  Were stilled with awe last night
            By the Northern Lights . . . .
                              that *Divine Spectacle.*

Resurrected Silent Stirrings

This essay previously appeared in 'The Journal of Pastoral Care & Counseling'
Vol. 59, Nos. 1-2, pp. 153-154
Spring-Summer
2005

Every other Wednesday morning I am privileged to facilitate a community of kindred spirits whose common denominator is a love for poetry. These twelve folks live in a nursing home. Together, we witness poetry giving voice to unspoken memories. It is an hour of pure grace. I have come to believe, as their chaplain, that the heaviest burdens we all carry are untold stories.

They congregate, most in wheelchairs, in a circle for "Poetry With the Pastor" to discuss both secular and Biblical poetry. There is no pressure to recite and no homework, just the sheer joy of being connected through listening and sharing. Interest soars when a line or word from a poem triggers a vivid memory. There is a fervent poetic spirit among the group. With schoolyard-like bonding, thoughts are exchanged after hearing the readings. Many mouth the words from memory as I read or recite. Those whose sight is dimmed listen attentively as the words paint richly detailed images in their minds. They are vicariously taken back to a nearly forgotten time and place in their routine lives.

"This poetry group brings back many of the lessons I taught my pupils many years ago in that one-room schoolhouse just down the road," says Lucy who is ninety-something. The poetry encourages communication by re-experiencing events through language, rhythm, metaphors, sounds, and images. It helps ease the aloneness that they all have in common. The poetry group is a safe place to share long-hidden stories.

The group sharing often proves healing for the risk-takers who share feelings that never before surfaced. Ella's comments were a balm to my own soul. "Good thoughts of my childhood come back a thousand times," said the 96-year-old after hearing Longfellow's "The Village Blacksmith." She proudly told the group, "My father was the best blacksmith in all of Hilltown Township." With tears, she articulated feelings of watching him work in his shop. "And I still miss him," she said in a whisper.

"The Daffodils" by Wordsworth, evokes thoughts of spring flowers. For Edna, it was a clear vision of mother on her knees in that bibbed calico apron with dirt-covered hands digging holes for the bulbs every fall. It was the annual mother-daughter sacred ritual that had to be done before the ground froze. Together, Edna and her mother would wait patiently for the resurrection of new life in the garden. "How Do I Love Thee? Let Me Count the Ways," that classic by Elizabeth Barrett Browning, evokes, for most, spontaneously shared reflections upon first loves.

That beloved Frost masterpiece, and my favorite, "The Road Not Taken," evokes fundamental truth telling to the listener. We humans invariably encounter life's vacillations. For contemplative Mable, it is about coming here to live. For this chaplain, a ministry with the elderly has indeed made all the difference in my life. I couldn't be surer of the ground whereupon the Holy Spirit put me to minister.

I thrive on hearing these gentle folk share their well-kept secret stories prompted by the poetry. Jane Kenyon was on the mark when pointing out, "One of the functions of poetry is to keep the memory of people and places and things and happenings alive." *(A Hundred White Daffodils, p. 164)*

These sages have become my mentors. They show me just how sacred the world is through their eyes and ears. The joy on their faces is contagious. Since girlhood, I have known that we all have a little poetry inside us waiting to come out. It is the way the spirit celebrates.

Observing these folks resurrect pieces of their living stories is like, for me, marveling with the surprised Mary at the tomb. The stone has been rolled away. The darkness has turned to radiant light, even for the dim-sighted. The dormant wisdom has finally sprung to life. Agonizing silences have been transformed into profound spoken words.

I must meekly confess, there are times when the poetry prompts me to discover and surface my own well-kept secrets . . . times when the stone rolls away and I confront those dark, hidden places in my own life and times when these gentle folk resurrect the silent stirrings in my own heart.

I am humbled and most richly blessed every other Wednesday morning by these resurrected silent stirrings.

About the Author

Dorothy Shelly has served as a chaplain in a faith based long-term care facility since 1996. Much of her ministry with the elderly centers on issues of loss, transition, and change. She is an ordained minister of the United Church of Christ. She is board certified by the Association of Professional Chaplains. She is past-president of the Pennsylvania Society of Chaplains and has had numerous poems published in professional periodicals.

Ministry is Dorothy's second career, having also enjoyed a professional life as a registered nurse. She earned an Associate Degree in Nursing from Montgomery County Community College, a Bachelor's Degree in Philosophy and Religion from Ursinus College and a Master of Divinity Degree from Lancaster Theological Seminary. Her background in nursing focused on gerontology, oncology, and mental health. She is presently pursuing Gestalt Pastoral Counseling.

Dorothy is a lover of poetry, a passionate perennial gardener, and an advocate for frequent get-a-ways to Vermont.

"Dorothy's poetry is a gift to each of us that transcends the rational and logical mind. Her poems reach deep into the recesses of the soul and invite us on a journey. The journey of our soul is witnessed and savored as we are engaged by her poetry. I find myself coming back to them again and again because they touch so deeply my own journey and the journey of those with whom I travel. Dorothy has put a delightful spiritual meal before us . . . come and eat."

—Roy Lewis, D.Min.
Chaplain to the Pine Run Community
Doylestown, PA

"This collection of poetic reflections captures both the pathos and the freedom of the human experience connected with illness and end of life issues. It resonates with Dot's ability to passionately be "with" the dying, those living in altered realities because of dementia and those who are seeking to discover who they are in the present moment now that they no longer are who they were. These poems are heart-wrenching, profound, mystically powerful, gentle, and compassionate. They reflect the human search for meaning, comfort, and hope. Her discovery of theology from within an Alzheimer's unit is our gift. I recommend this book for all who minister to others no matter where they are on the continuum of living and dying."

—Rhoda Glick, M.Div.
Gestalt Pastoral Care minister
Lancaster, PA

"Dorothy Shelly knows what a poet needs to know. She listens first. Then she finds the truest and most direct words to the heart of the matter. She notices the small details that most of us would miss because we are too busy analyzing the situation—whether theologically or psychologically. We might have missed what she sees clearly in a random remark, a cry, a tear or a sigh. She takes these sacred moments and gives them a texture rooted in the symbolism of faith and the certainty of God's loving embrace when minds and hearts finally fail. These are vignettes of pastoral attentiveness which are not so much focused on the chaplain—poet as they are on the patients yielding up their truth and having it received by someone ready to translate its meaning into language we might well hear ourselves."

—Frank J. Stalfa, Jr.
Professor of Pastoral Theology
Lancaster Theological Seminary